This book belongs to:

MONSTER DOODLES

For Kids

CHRIS SABATINO

GIBBS SMITH
TO ENRICH AND INSPIRE HUMANKIND

Manufactured in Altona, Manitoba, Canada in
September 2011 by Friesen

First Edition
15 14 13 12 11   15 14 13 12 11 10 9 8 7 6 5 4 3

Text © 2011 by Chris Sabatino
Illustrations © 2011 by Chris Sabatino

Published by
Gibbs Smith
P.O. Box 667
Layton, Utah 84041

1.800.835.4993 orders
www.gibbs-smith.com

Designed by Renee Bond

Gibbs Smith books are printed on either
recycled, 100% post-consumer waste, FSC-
certified papers or on paper produced from
sustainable PEFC-certified forest/controlled
wood source. Learn more at www.pefc.org.

ISBN: 978-1-4236-2020-4

Draw the thing that goes bump in the night!

Draw yourself as a
monster slayer.

Self portrait of my inner monster!

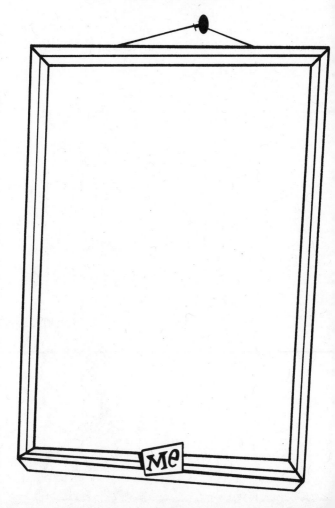

The monster he's hiding from is right behind him. Draw it.

Draw the alien bursting from this guy's stomach!

What does the vampire's castle look like?

Something horrible is outside the shower curtain. Draw its outline!

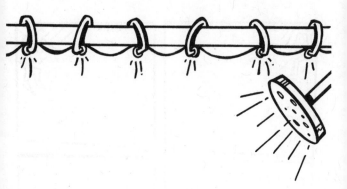

Who or what is lurking outside the window?

Give these creatures some scary faces.

Draw frightened faces on these humans.

Yikes! It's a zombie!

Draw a stink monster jumping out of this locker.

What does the dust demon under your bed look like?

Draw the creature that lives in your closet.

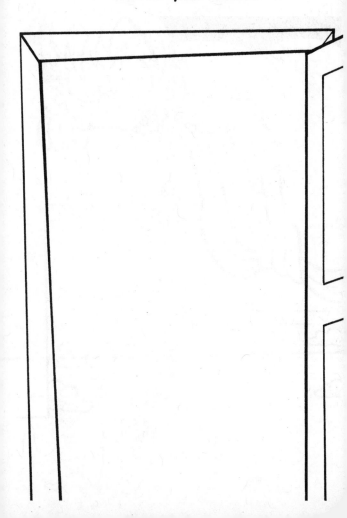

What is the mad scientist creating?

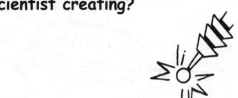

Fill this jar with monster brains.

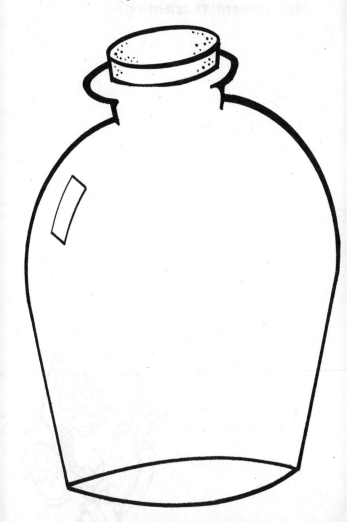

A giant piranha fish is eating this science teacher. Draw it.

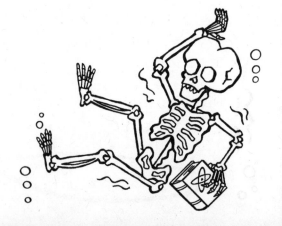

Something is dragging this kid underwater.

What did they find on Planet Gruesome?

Giant space worms are invading the space station!

Who's on the back of this motorcycle?

Give this beast some tattoos.

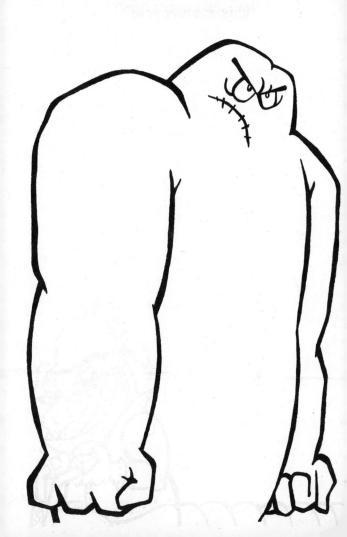

Can you draw an invisible monster?

Close your eyes and draw
a wild maniac here.

Draw a dinosaur that all the others are afraid of.

What's inside this prehistoric egg?

Draw the creature from your neighbor's pool.

Draw a Zombie Scout selling zombie cookies.

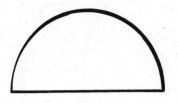

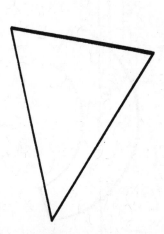

Turn these shapes into
mini monsters.

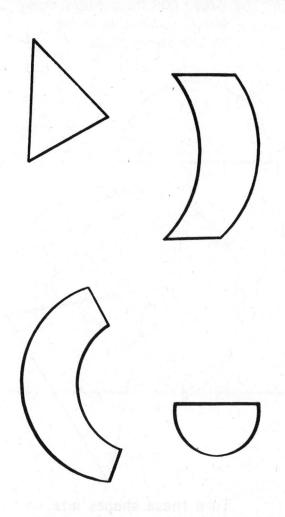

The world can be a frightening
place. Turn this globe
into a scary monster.

Draw the nervous freak
in your stomach!

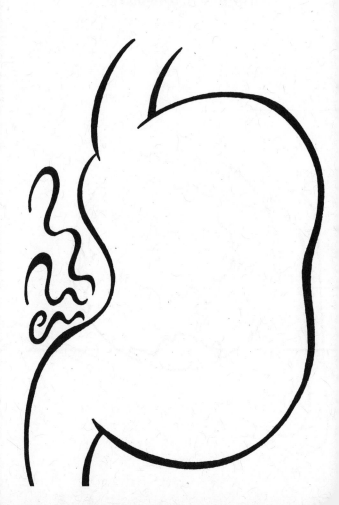

Two creatures are in
the car's backseat.

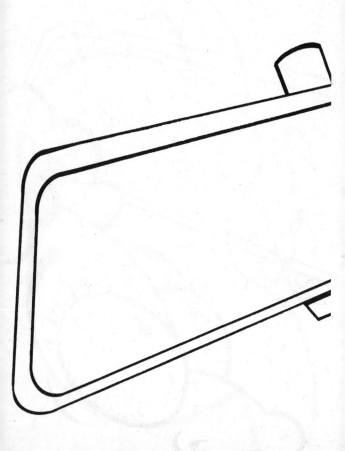

Draw them in the
rearview mirror.

Here's the daddy.
Draw the "mummy."

The Statue of Liberty is battling a flying turtle of terror!

A big SCREAM TV is taking over TV Town!

Draw the <u>real</u> creature
that is behind this kid at
a 3-D monster movie.

Give this ogre a scary weapon.

Draw the rest of this ghoul.

MONSTER
PARTS
SALE

Create a monster using
some of the body parts
on the other page.

What gives you goose bumps?

This is why people are afraid of the dark!

Draw the bottom halves
of these creatures.

What's in this shark's mouth?

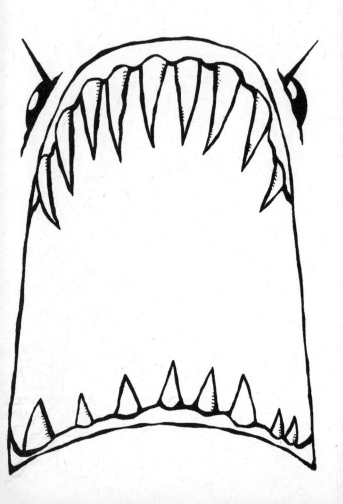

It's a fire-breathing dragon!

Hello, giant ants! Goodbye, picnic!

Draw the earthworm beast that's about to bite this kid on the behind!

The vampire's dog is a
bloodhound. Draw it.

What do you feed this creature created in science class?

**What kind of monster
would have these teeth?**

Draw the rest of the
creature with these eyes.

What's creeping out of this grave?

Put a face on this demon clown.

The ponytail has turned into a spine-chilling hair horror!

Draw a man-eating monster!

Draw Snow Fright's seven monsters.

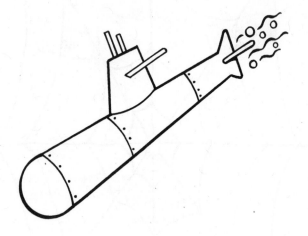

A giant jellyfish is attacking
this submarine!

Draw a creepy giant
spider in the web.

What is Larry saying as he changes into a werewolf?

Larry has completed the change.
What does he look like now?

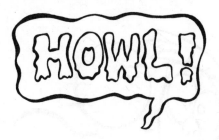

Draw the thing that's escaped the video game!

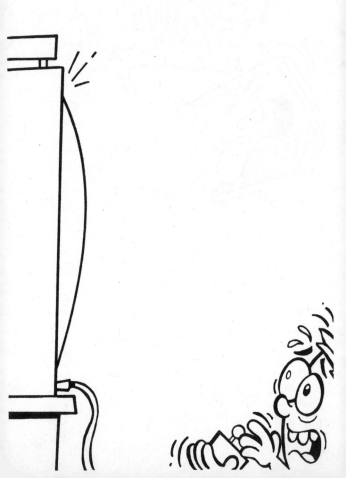

The infected laptop is throwing up a computer virus!

**What frightens you on
Friday the 13th?**

Design the scariest
Halloween costume ever!

Game cancelled due to fire-breathing, flying pigs!

Escaped mummy ruins the museum field trip!

Something in the basement grabbed your foot!

Draw your worst nightmare ever!

Draw a hungry vampire
making a withdrawal.

Fill in the monster's X-ray.

Turn this happy family into a group of undead zombies.

Draw the guts of this mechanical monster.

Billy's robot invention is destroying the science fair!

**Finish the rest of this
robot dinosaur.**

What's creeping out of this cave?

There's a troll under this bridge.

Draw a hunchback wearing this heavy backpack.

Create a fire alien on the surface of Mercury.

Draw the abominable snowman on this snowy cliff.

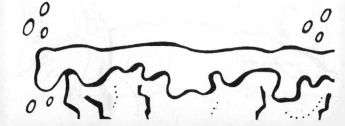

Eating curds and whey has turned Little Miss Muffet into Little Miss Monster!

All the king's men put Humpty Dumpty together all wrong!

Turn these shapes into haunting spooks.

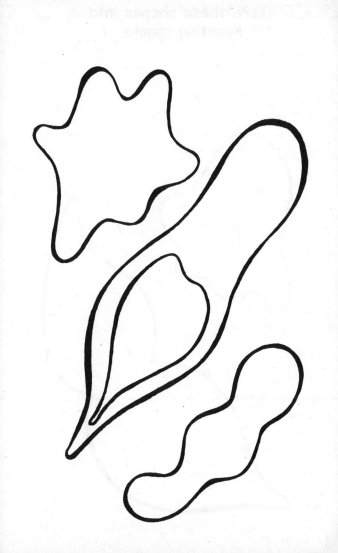

Create a creature completely from your imagination.

Draw a monster someone describes to you.

A giant Venus Flytrap is about to eat the cafeteria lady!

There's a moldy monster in the back of the fridge!

Serve up some sinister
singing spinach.

Cook up a monster
mash-ed potato.

Draw a monster twister tornado.

Bigfoot is dancing in
a ballet recital.

A mobster lobster is making
his getaway on water skis.

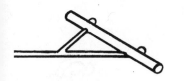

Watch out! A giant, mutant fly!

The bed bugs are biting. Draw them.

Your imaginary friend is back . . . and evil!

What do zombies have nightmares about?

Who's sneaking up on the babysitter?

What creature are the angry villagers chasing?

Who is coming out of the coffin?

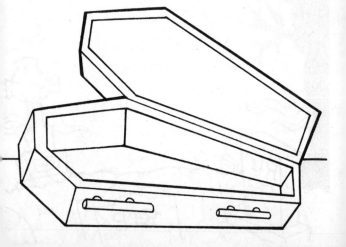

Who is in the spooky cemetery?

What does the fortune teller see in the crystal ball?

The candle smoke is turning into a ghost!

Jimmy's scout tent is filled with bats!

Johnny's tent is filled with snakes!

WORST CAMPING TRIP EVER!

What's he thinking?

What's she saying?

Draw the front part of this sea serpent.

Give this squid beast some arms.

Name this super team of monsters.

Draw a new member
for the team.

Angry bears are waking up Goldilocks!

Little Red Riding Hood meets the wicked wolf!

What is the evil ventriloquist dummy saying?

The teddy bear is possessed by a demon!

Draw the invading aliens.

Draw the alien pet.

Redraw this vampire as a bat.

**Dr. Jekyll looks in the mirror
and sees evil Mr. Hyde!**

Draw the phantom of the oatmeal.

The stomach ache monster is attacking!

The time machine has brought a creature from the past!

Draw a monster of the future.

What's lurking at the end of your bed?

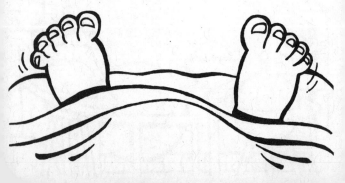

What does fear look like to you?

Finish the rest of this Cyclops.

Draw five heads on this
five-headed monster.

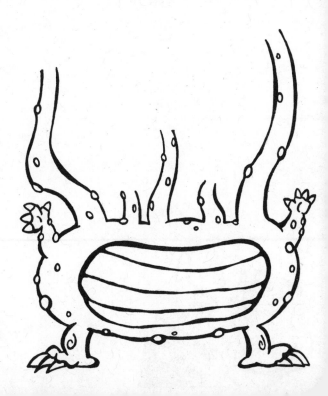

Draw a scene from a monster movie.

What's captured
the princess?

The prince has been turned
into a freaky frog.

Scariest birthday present ever.

Draw a soccer monster.

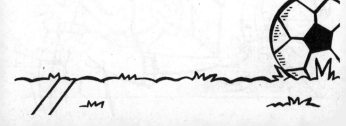

Draw a ghost writer.

Make Mr. Gray's picture age before your eyes!

What book could be this scary?

Most frightening movie ever made.

What's this zombie cowboy riding?

Create a creepy cactus creature.

A creature is destroying your school!

What monster would steal candy from a baby?

Shark!

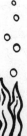

Flying freak!

Turn this letter M
into a monster.

Make a crazy creature from
the letters in your name.

You're playing monster
cards. Draw the joker.

Design a monster trap.

Ugly lamp. Evil genie!

There's a witch in the spelling bee!

Giant blob of tapioca pudding invades the cafeteria!

Evil dodge balls attack during gym class!

Draw a haunted tree.

ITS BITE iS WORSE THAN iTS BARK.

A creature is coming out of the swamp!

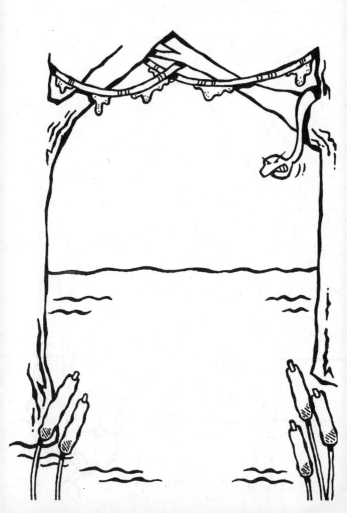

There's a mini monster in the pocket!

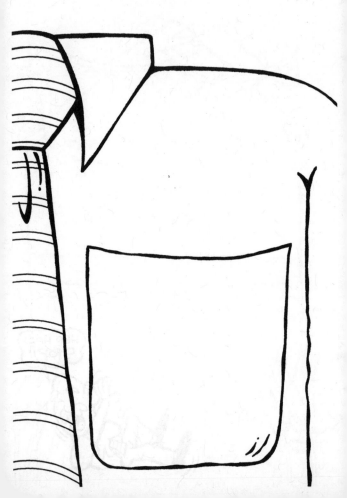

Draw a tickle monster.

He was swallowed by a giant
whale. Draw his new home.

Evil electric eel!

Draw a haunted house.

There's something creepy in the haunted house!

Create artwork for the Monster Museum.

Scariest jack-o-lanterns ever!

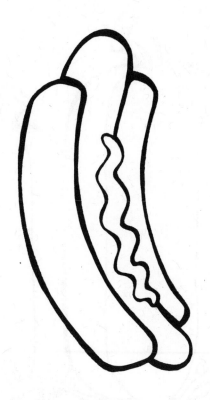

Turn this hotdog into a Halloweenie.

Draw trolls making
Troll House Cookies.

Draw goblins gobbling down the cookies.

A ghost is rockin' to your MP3 player!

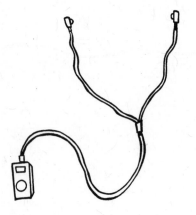

In this graveyard, skeletons dance after midnight.

Draw the beast they're hiding from.

What big brute is breaking through this brick wall?

A jungle beast is flipping out the jungle boy!

She's a half-wicked old witch!

He's only half werewolf!

Draw a rock & roll creature.

It's a sinister, surfing freak!

Draw the troll toll collector.

Draw the eerie grave digger.

What's in the upper bunk?

It's the creature
from the lagoon.

Create a candy bar only a dinosaur would like.

What do ogres have for breakfast?

Create a creature completely
out of triangles.

Quick! Draw a scribble monster.

Draw a ghost ship.

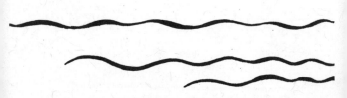

What's on Terror Island?

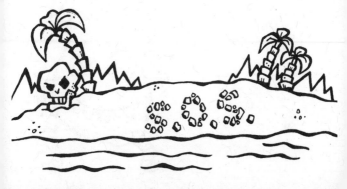

How do you get rid of
a potato monster?

Something scary is on the couch.

There are tiny terrors in his hair!

Draw a cavity creature.

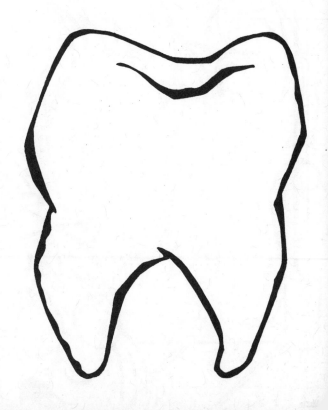

It's a dark and stormy night.
Who is lurking in the shadows?

Change the clouds into wild demons.

Draw a head on this alien.

Give the creature a body.

Draw the newspaper photo.

What's on the cover?

Draw a giant that likes lemonade.

What do monsters sell?

A monster rabbit is trying to saw the magician in half!

What horror did the witch create?

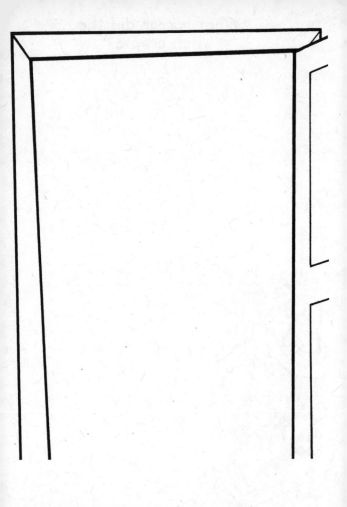

Knock! Knock! It's the boogeyman!

Draw what gives you the creeps.

The evil pillow is attacking!

EEK! Monster prints all over the bedroom.

The melted mutant has escaped the volcano!

Draw an icicle creature that gives you the shivers.

Robot Monster forgot his head
because it wasn't screwed on.

The dog catcher captured
a baby werewolf.

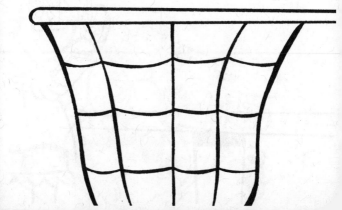

The kitty litter creature has escaped the box!

Evil fire hydrant! Draw
a frightened dog.

Draw the monster clubhouse.

Draw a ghost town.

Trapped in the elevator
with a heavy horror!

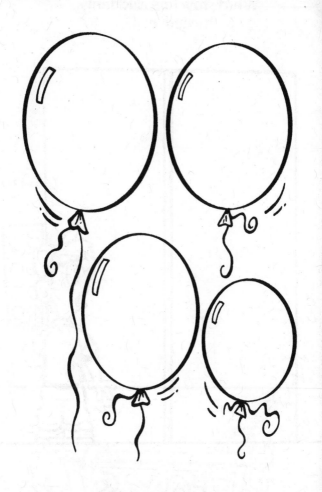

Make evil faces on these balloons.

What toy has suddenly turned evil?

A garbage ghoul lives
in the dumpster.

Draw the beast that flings this tail.

Make the evil wizard, who wears this hat, appear.

What's escaping from the sewer?

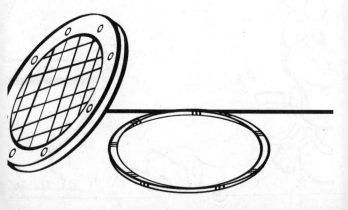

A giant alligator is coming out of the toilet!

Draw the Space Monster
Patrol spaceship.

Draw the space monster the patrol officer is shooting at!

Create a freak made of rocks.

Draw a beast made of slime.

Draw the ghost family's car.

I bet you're itching to draw
a poison ivy monster!

Aren't you dying to draw
the king of the zombies?

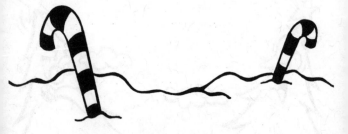

Draw an evil elf . . .

and his fiendish flying reindeer!

Mack the monster is driving a monster truck. Draw it.

Something's coming
down the chimney.

Beware! Hitchhiking corpse!

What did they see on the Tunnel of Horrors ride?

The crispy bacon creature is fighting the devilish egg monster!

Revenge of the
Thanksgiving turkey!

Draw what's at the bottom
of the Dead Sea.

What did the vampire catch in Lake Eerie?

An alien is hitching a ride
on this space shuttle.

What on earth is shocking this alien visitor?

Draw a mean monster librarian.

Create a demon dentist.

Draw whatever horror
you like here.

Draw a bicycle built
for two creatures.

This creepy creature painting has come to life!

A monster is the artist.

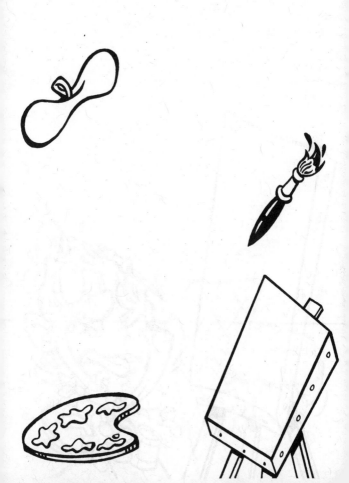

Create an I scream flavor.

Draw this monster baby's bizarre rattle.

Make this HEXagon into
a witch's face.

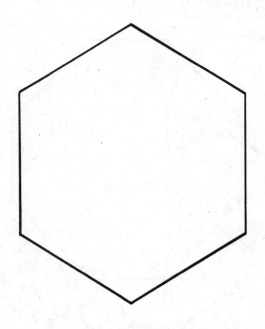

This OCTagon is a giant OCTopus.

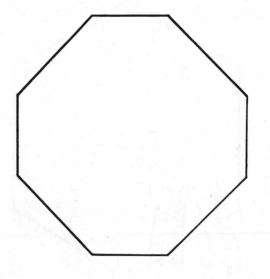

Draw the rest of these monsters.

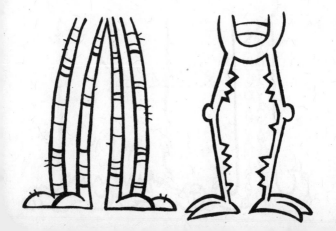

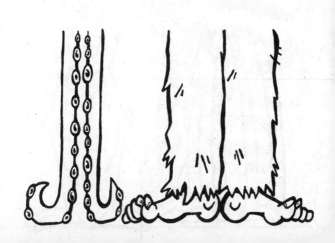

What do monsters doodle?

Draw a family of hairy beasts.

The
Beasty
Bunch

What's on the Saturday afternoon monster movie?

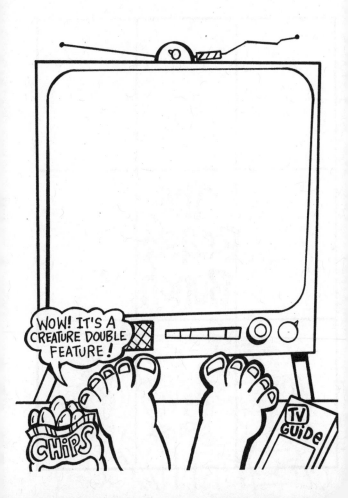

A real monster is creeping up behind these trick-or-treaters!